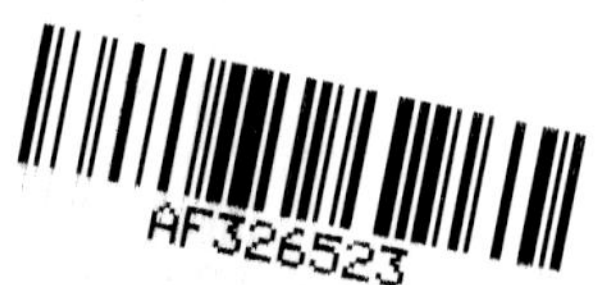
AF326523

Effortlessness

|

Paradox